Moomba

T0362854

Melbourne's Festival

It is the festival.

3

There is a lot to do at the festival.

There is face painting at the festival.

We can make big bubbles at the festival.

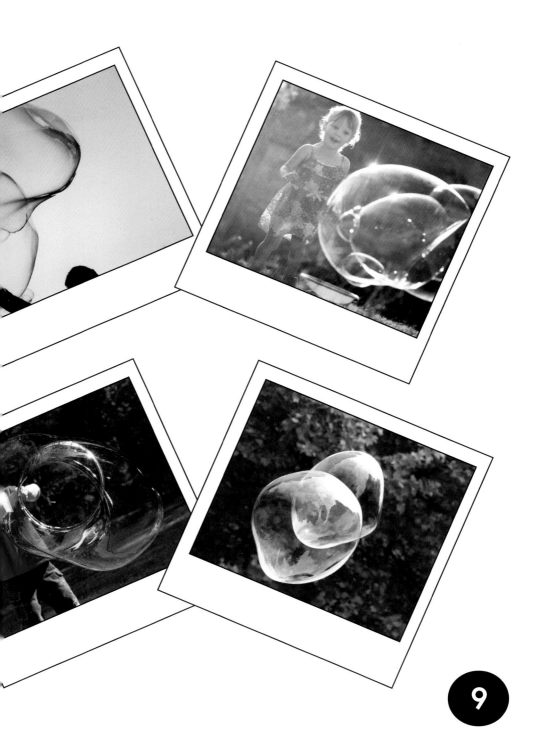

We can go on rides at the festival.

There is a parade
at the festival.

There are fireworks at the festival.

We will have fun
at the festival.